CRISIS IN THE CARIBBEAN

VANISHING RESOURCES

HERBERT BUCHSBAUM

Steck-Vaughn™

A Harcourt Achieve Imprint

www.Steck-Vaughn.com
1-800-531-5015

Crisis in the Caribbean: Vanishing Resources
By Herbert Buchsbaum

Photo Acknowledgements
Cover ©Edmond Van Hoorick/SuperStock; t.o.c. ©Manu Sassoonian/
Art Resource, NY; p. 5 Jacques Descloitres, MODIS Rapid Response
Team, NASA/GSFC; p. 7 ©CORBIS; p. 9 ©Bildarchiv Preussischer
Kulturbesitz/Art Resource, NY; p. 10 ©The Granger Collection,
New York; p. 12 courtesy Angela Morel; p. 12 courtesy Alix Almonord;
p. 15 ©Bob Strong/The Image Works; p. 17 ©MARK EDWARDS/
Peter Arnold, Inc.; p. 19 ©Manu Sassoonian/Art Resource, NY; p. 23
©Catherine Karnow/CORBIS; p. 25 ©Tony Arruza/CORBIS; p. 27
©Reuters/CORBIS.

ISBN 1-4190-2291-1

Printed in the United States of America

1 2 3 4 5 6 7 8 152 12 11 10 09 08 07 06 05

TABLE OF CONTENTS

"The Fairest Land"

INTRODUCTION

In 1492, Christopher Columbus sailed from Spain. He crossed the Atlantic Ocean looking for Asia. Instead, he landed on a beautiful island in a New World. White sand beaches stretched for miles. Thick green forests covered the island. Pink flamingos flew across clear blue lakes.

Columbus was amazed. "This is the **fairest** land under heaven," he wrote.

He named the island Hispaniola, or "Little Spain." On it, he built the first permanent European **settlement** in the Americas.

Europeans moved to the island. They hunted for gold. They planted crops in the rich soil. For years, Hispaniola produced great wealth, but not for its natives.

Hispaniola sits in the middle of the Caribbean Sea, just 700 miles southeast of Florida. In the 1800s, it split into two countries, Haiti and the Dominican Republic.

Today, most of the island's wealth is gone. Hispaniola ranks among the poorest places in the world. It has suffered many wars. Its wealth has been stolen by **dictators**. Its forests have been cut and burned.

Every year, thousands of people leave the island. There are too few jobs there. Many people **emigrate** in search of opportunities in the United States.

In this book, you'll meet two young people who made that journey. You'll also learn about the two halves of the island they left behind.

CHAPTER 1

History of an Island

Before 1492, the island was a home to the Taino. More than 300,000 of them lived there. They fished and hunted. They grew corn, sweet potatoes, and squash. They lived in small huts made of palm leaves and straw. They had never seen a white person before.

In December of that year, Columbus and his crew arrived. The island was never the same again. The Taino called their home *Ayti*. It meant "land of mountains." Columbus called it Hispaniola. He had another name for the Taino, too. It was based on a mistake. He thought he had landed near India. So, he called them Indians.

In 1496, the Spanish built the town of Santo Domingo. Over the next two centuries, thousands of Spanish settlers arrived. European rule **expanded** throughout the Caribbean. Soon, Spain controlled much of present-day Central America. Hispaniola was their first base. Today, it is the oldest European-built town in the New World.

The Taino greeted Columbus with gifts.

Columbus liked the Taino. "There is no better nor gentler people in the world," he wrote. The Spanish had plans for the island, though. They hoped to find gold in its streams and mountainsides. They wanted to produce crops for **export** to Spain. The settlers needed people to do the work. So, they forced the Taino into slavery.

The Taino resisted with bows and arrows. The Spanish had guns. Spanish soldiers forced the Taino into hard **labor**. They made the Taino hunt for gold, cut down the forests for wood, and plant sugarcane. Many of the laborers died. Some tried to flee. If they did, they were hunted down with dogs. However, many Taino died of the new diseases the Spanish had brought with them. These diseases were common in Europe. The Taino had no natural **immunity** to them. By 1550, only 150 Taino were left.

The Spanish needed new slaves to work on the **plantations** and to mine for gold. That's how Africans came to the island. Slave traders captured or bought slaves on the west coast of Africa. They sold them in Hispaniola. African slave labor built most of the colony.

In the 1600s, the Spanish had rivals. Portugal, France, and England saw Spain's new riches. These countries wanted a share of the New World's **resources**. They sent explorers west to claim new territories.

In Hispaniola, Spanish settlements clustered in the east near Santo Domingo. That left the western half of the island free for other countries to **colonize**.

By the 1780s, more than 500,000 people lived on Hispaniola. Nearly 90 percent of them were slaves.

Pirates also lived on Hispaniola. They raided **merchant** ships in the Caribbean Sea. Little by little, the French kicked most of the pirates out. In 1697, France took over the western third of the island.

The French colony grew rich quickly. Besides sugar, it produced coffee and cotton. The French brought more slaves from Africa. Hundreds of thousands of African men and women worked the fields. In the late 1700s, the island was the richest colony in the New World.

Then, in 1791, the African slaves rebelled against the French. They outnumbered their masters by almost ten-to-one. In August, 100,000 slaves burned down plantations and executed slave owners.

An army of former slaves defeated the French and Spanish to help establish an independent Haiti.

A freed slave named François Toussaint L'Ouverture had trained the rebels. He turned them into expert soldiers. Eventually, Toussaint and his army defeated both the French and Spanish armies. After that, they ruled the whole island. Later, the French sent 20,000 troops to retake Hispaniola. The rebels held them off. In 1804, they created an independent government and **abolished** slavery.

The African leaders wanted to pay respect to the Taino. So, they used the native name for the island. They called their country Haiti.

Haiti became the second independent country in the Americas. (The United States was the first.) It was also the first black **republic** in the world. In 1844, the Spanish area in the east won independence from Haiti. It became the Dominican Republic. From then on, the island would be home to two nations.

CULTURAL SOUP

Both Haiti and the Dominican Republic owe a lot to their African and European past. The Haitian **Creole** language is a mixture of French and African words. Dominican **salsa** dancing comes from a mixture of European and African dance.

In both countries, African and European religions mingled. The Europeans were Roman Catholic. Many slaves became Catholic, too. They also kept some of their African beliefs. **Voodoo** means "spirit" in a West African language. Many Haitians attend both Catholic church and voodoo ceremonies.

Today, Hispaniola's cultural traditions are alive and well. However, the island's **economic** wealth is gone. **Poverty** touches the lives of most people on the island.

Meet Angela and Alix

Angela Morel and Alix Almonord both grew up in small towns. They lived less than 100 miles apart. Still, they came from very different **cultures**.

Angela speaks Spanish. She loves to dance to salsa music. Alix speaks Creole, a form of French. He listens to **zouk**, a Creole dance music.

Both Angela and Alix grew up on Hispaniola. It's a small island, about the size of South Carolina. Yet, it's home to two countries. Angela lived on the east side, in the Dominican Republic. The Dominican Republic was a Spanish **colony**. Its language, food, music, and traditions are mostly Spanish.

Angela Morel came from the Dominican Republic at age 12. She's now a junior in high school. Alix Almonord now attends college in New York. He moved to the United States from Haiti when he was 17.

Alix lived on the west side, in Haiti. Haiti was a French colony. Most Haitians are the descendants of African slaves. Their traditions are a mix of French and African **customs**.

Despite their differences, Angela and Alix have one thing in common. Their parents moved to the United States for the same reason. They wanted a better life for themselves and their children.

In Haiti, Alix's family had a hard life. To earn money, his mother walked horses across the border to the Dominican Republic. There, she bought 50-gallon drums of gasoline. She strapped them onto the animals. Then, she brought them home to sell to gas stations. It was difficult and dangerous work. Still, she could barely support Alix and his four brothers and sisters.

Angela's parents also worked hard. Her father pumped gas at a filling station. Her mother worked in an office.

Both families eventually moved to New York City. Alix came when he was 17. Angela moved when she was 12. They have started new lives. They have big plans. Still, they haven't forgotten the island they used to call home. They each want to help their homeland in the future.

Haiti: Caribbean Desert

In Haiti, Alix Almonord and his family lived in a one-room apartment. When it rained, water poured in through the roof. They had no running water or electricity. They had no car. They didn't even own a bicycle. As the youngest child, Alix shared a bed with his mother and sister. The family often had one meal a day. Sometimes it was just a bowl of rice and beans. Most days, Alix had no money for lunch.

Luckily, Alix was good in math. It was a skill he could sell in the schoolyard. In exchange for helping with math, Alix would get money or an orange.

"That was my lunch," Alix says. "I was lucky. I could trade knowledge for food."

Cite Soleil is Haiti's largest slum. Several hundred thousand people live there in extreme poverty.

Many Haitians aren't as lucky as Alix. More than 80 percent of Haiti's people live in poverty.

About 70 percent of Haitians have no jobs. Millions of people live in vast **slums**. Their homes are shacks made out of tin or cardboard.

Half the Haitian population can't read or write. Even public schools cost money to attend. Families have to buy books and uniforms. Most can't afford it. Alix's family usually had money to send him to school. Still, one day he was sent home because he didn't have his history book. His family didn't have the money to buy it. Alix went home and cried.

Money Trouble

What has happened to Haiti in the last 200 years? When Haiti's African leaders created their own government, they still were not completely free. France forced Haiti to pay for recognition as an independent nation. That meant the new government had little money left.

In addition, the Haitians had abolished slavery. Without slave labor, the plantations didn't make money. Haitians still grew crops, but their farms were small. The farmers didn't produce enough food to export to other countries. Exporting goods brings money into a country. Without that money, Haiti had to borrow heavily from foreign countries.

The next problem was political. Haiti's revolution against France lasted 13 years. The long war nearly ruined Haiti. The country's leaders were given a lot of power to restore order. They wrote a constitution that let the president rule for life. The president became a dictator, as did those after him.

Haiti continued to borrow money from other nations. They could have built factories or modernized farms, but Haiti's dictators stole most of the money. As a result, the country's economy failed to grow.

As Haiti slid deeper into debt, its environment was ruined. The problem stems from Haiti having few power plants. Since there is little electricity, people burn

Haiti has less than 2 percent of its forests left.

charcoal for energy. The charcoal is made from wood. Poor people cut down trees so they can make and sell charcoal. It's one of the few ways to earn a living.

Without trees, the soil **erodes**, or washes away. Without good soil, crops fail. Farmers give up their farms and move to the cities to find work. Most people can't find jobs. To make money, they cut more trees. The **vicious cycle** begins again.

When Columbus landed, three-quarters of Haiti was covered with trees. Today, 98.5 percent of those trees are gone. Every year, Haitians cut down 15 to 20 million trees. As a result, the island loses about 36 million tons of **topsoil** a year. Once lush and green, Haiti is becoming the first desert in the Caribbean.

THE RICH GET RICHER

The dictators made themselves rich while the Haitians suffered. Today, the country's wealth is shared by a small number of **elite** families. Armed guards look after their **mansions** and their swimming pools. Expensive cars sit in their driveways. They send their children to private schools in Europe.

When Alix was little, the Duvalier family ruled Haiti. François Duvalier was dictator from 1957 to 1971. He was called Papa Doc. Then, his son Jean-Claude, known as Baby Doc, took over. The Duvaliers started their own police force. They were called the Tonton Macoutes, a Creole term that means "bogeymen." They wore dark sunglasses and bandanas. They carried big knives called machetes. The Macoutes jailed and **tortured** opponents of the Duvaliers.

Many Haitians tried to flee the poverty and violence. In the 1970s and 1980s, thousands of people climbed onto homemade rafts. They tried to paddle the 700 miles to Florida. Many died at sea. Others were caught by the U.S. Coast Guard and sent back.

Finally, in 1990, Haiti held its first free elections. A Catholic priest named Jean-Bertrand Aristide became president. He promised to rebuild Haiti's schools and clean up the slums.

Aristide became a hero to the poor. Alix's mother joined his political party. "Aristide was a kind of promise to the country," Alix says. "He was full of promise and change."

Unfortunately, former soldiers took over the country again in 2004. Aristide was forced to flee. By then, however, Alix had moved to the United States.

There are signs of hope in Haiti. Aristide made people realize that democracy is possible. International groups are working to help save Haiti's environment. The U.S. Agency for International Development (USAID) has planted 60 million trees in the last twenty years. Other groups are trying to get Haitians to use solar energy or propane gas instead of charcoal.

Someday, Alix hopes to go back to Haiti. He thinks he can help the country pull itself out of poverty.

Haitians are known for their colorful artwork.

"My hope is to make Haiti more democratic."

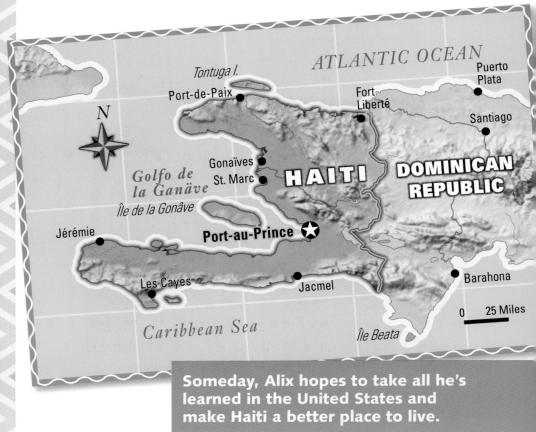

Someday, Alix hopes to take all he's learned in the United States and make Haiti a better place to live.

In 1999, when he was 17, Alix moved to the United States. He left his friends and his heart in Haiti.

I grew up in Fort Liberté, a city in northeastern Haiti. We were never poor by Haitian standards. For Haiti, we were middle class.

On weekends we would go to the country. We would pick mangos and eat them. Then we'd go to the river and swim. We'd come back and eat sugarcane. By six o'clock, we would pack our bags and go home. That's what I loved to do on the weekend. If you don't do that, you feel like you've had a bad weekend.

When my mom told me we were leaving Haiti, I didn't want to go at all. It was very difficult to leave my friends. I still dream about some of them. My friends and I were like a family. We would go on our own after school.

We would share food together. I almost never ate with my family. And we would study together. I'm good at math, but I'm a dummy at spelling, so we would help each other.

I'm happy in the U.S. I'm **fortunate** that I have more resources here. I go to college now. I want to be remembered as a scientist. I want to discover a new element in the periodic table. Or, maybe be the next Einstein.

If I can be a good citizen here and get educated here, that's a hope for Haiti. With my education, I hope to go back to Haiti. My hope is to make Haiti more democratic.

Dominican Republic: Sugar Shock

CHAPTER 3

Angela Morel has fond memories of the Dominican Republic. Her family wasn't wealthy, but they lived comfortably. Their home was out in the country. "We had a house with a big porch," Angela says. "We had roses in front. We had lemon, cherry, and plantain trees in back."

One day, Angela saw the other side of life in the Dominican Republic. She went to visit a friend after school. The friend lived with her very poor aunt in a tin shack. "When I saw how she lived, I started crying," Angela says. "I didn't understand why I lived in a house and she didn't. When I saw that, my heart was broken apart."

Rising prices and lack of jobs have sent many Dominicans fleeing to the United States in search of a better life.

Like Haiti, the Dominican Republic has plenty of tin shacks. It ranks as one of the poorest countries in the world. In recent years, the situation has gotten worse. Prices have risen fast. Unemployment has also risen. More than half of all Dominicans live in poverty. Many of them, like Angela's family, have fled to the United States looking for work.

A Different Path

Dominicans, in some ways, are better off than their neighbors in Haiti. You can see the **contrast** between the two countries when you fly over the island. From a plane, Haiti looks brown. The ground is either bone dry or muddy. Farther east, over the Dominican Republic, parts still look lush and green. Why? The reason lies in the island's history.

In the 1700s, the Spaniards who lived in the Dominican Republic didn't run as many large plantations. Spanish farmers weren't forced to grow sugar like their French neighbors in Haiti. And so, they didn't need to import as many slaves as the French. The Spanish harvested a variety of crops from smaller farms. Many became cattle ranchers. So, when slavery was banned, not much changed on the Spanish side of the island. They could keep the economy going.

In the late 1800s, the Dominican economy changed. Small farms began to disappear. Large sugar plantations were more **profitable**. Like Haiti, the Dominican Republic suffered through wars and dictatorships.

In 1930, Rafael Trujillo took over as dictator. He ran the country for more than thirty years. He had his own secret police. They operated much like the Tonton Macoutes in Haiti. They spied on people. They jailed or even killed those who spoke out against them.

The Dominican Republic's main export is sugar.

Under Trujillo, the Dominican economy grew. Yet, only a few people benefited. Trujillo took over many of the country's sugar, coffee, and cocoa plantations. He gave high-paying jobs to his friends and relatives. A small number of people grew very wealthy. Most Dominicans stayed poor. Finally, Trujillo was killed in 1961.

In the 1980s, disaster struck. The Dominican Republic depended on soft drink companies to buy its sugar. Then, soft drink companies started using corn syrup to sweeten their sodas. They stopped buying sugar.

25

The Dominican economy crashed. Plantations shut down. Sugar refineries closed. Many Dominicans suffered. People lost their jobs. Meanwhile, everything from food to gas to housing got more expensive.

Angela's parents still had jobs. Yet, it was harder to put food on the table. Angela remembers how **inflation** affected her. A bag of potato chips cost five pesos one month. Soon after, it cost fifteen. "I was shocked," she says. Many families decided that they could no longer support themselves in their country.

Dominicans left the country in huge numbers. Most of them fled to the United States. Today, 8.8 million Dominicans live in the Dominican Republic. Another one million live in the United States. Nearly 600,000 of them live in New York City. Only Santo Domingo, the capital of the Dominican Republic, has a larger Dominican population.

Today, Angela is proud of the country she left behind. Since 1996, the Dominican Republic has held free and fair elections. Its economy grew quickly in the late 1990s. One of the country's biggest sources of income comes from its emigrants. Dominicans in the U.S. now send home about $2 billion a year. The money gives many families a much better lifestyle than they would have otherwise.

Dominican baseball star Sammy Sosa has helped many Dominicans back home. He built a medical center there. In 1998, a huge hurricane hit the Dominican Republic. Sosa raised millions to help the survivors.

Angela is now in high school in New York City. She knows she has an opportunity most kids at home don't have. She's determined, like Sosa, to use that opportunity to help others.

Nearly 400 Dominicans have played major league baseball in the states. Home-run king Sammy Sosa is one of them.

"I feel proud to be a Dominican."

When Angela finishes school, she wants to apply her skills to help others in her native country.

Angela came to New York City when she was 12. She had to start her life again.

When I got my visa to come to the U.S., I was so excited. When I got here, I realized I would have to learn a new language. I would have to make new friends again.

I will never forget my first day of school in the U.S. I went to my principal, and I was afraid to open my mouth. I was afraid I would say something that was not correct, and he was going to laugh at me. And when I entered the classroom, all the kids stared at me. I just wanted the earth to eat me. I was so afraid.

The next day, I didn't want to go to school. Every day when I had to do my homework, I would cry. I just didn't understand it. In my English class, I tried to hide under my desk so the teacher wouldn't call on me.

Still, I worked hard to learn English. Now I'm doing well in school. After high school, I want to go to college. I want to be a professional, maybe a lawyer or a **psychologist**. If you're a psychologist, you can help people with mental illness. Being a lawyer, you can help get justice for people.

I feel like I'm 100 percent Dominican. Even though my country isn't as good as I want it to be, I feel proud to be Dominican. I feel proud of what I am. You cannot say you're American if the blood in your veins is Caribbean. But what makes a person isn't just your nationality. What makes a person is what you are. Your word, what you stand for, that's you.

abolish (*verb*) to get rid of

colonize (*verb*) to settle and rule another land

colony (*noun*) land that is under the control of another country

contrast (*noun*) to be very different from something else

Creole (*noun*) a French-based language

culture (*noun*) a group of people's way of life

custom (*noun*) a tradition common to a community

dictator (*noun*) a ruler of a country or government who has total power over the people

economic (*adjective*) having to do with a country's wealth and industry

elite (*adjective*) a group of people who have more education, money, or power than others

emigrate (*verb*) to leave a country and live elsewhere

erode (*verb*) to wash away

expand (*verb*) to make larger or add to

export (*verb*) to sell goods to another country

fairest (*adjective*) the most beautiful

fortunate (*adjective*) to be lucky; to have good fortune

immunity (*noun*) the body's ability to resist a disease

inflation (*noun*) a rise in prices when the same amount of money buys less

labor (*noun*) hard work, taking lots of effort

mansion (*noun*) a large, expensive house

merchant (*adjective*) related to the buying or selling of goods

plantation (*noun*) a large farm where one main crop is grown, such as sugar or cotton

poverty (*noun*) the state of being poor

profitable (*adjective*) having the ability to make money

psychologist (*noun*) a person trained to help people figure out personal problems

republic (*noun*) a nation with voting citizens

resources (*noun*) the available money, labor, or raw materials of a country

salsa (*noun*) a kind of Latin-American dance music

settlement (*noun*) a place people set up to live

slum (*noun*) a poor and overcrowded living area

torture (*verb*) to abuse physically

topsoil (*noun*) the upper layer of soil which is the richest for growing plants

vicious cycle (*noun*) problems leading to other problems

Voodoo (*noun*) a Haitian religion that mixes African beliefs and Catholicism

zouk (*noun*) a kind of Haitian dance music

IDIOMS

wanted the earth to eat me (*page 29*) embarrassed or scared; to want to disappear
When the teacher called me to the chalkboard, I just wanted the earth to eat me.